C.L. Chan

SABAH COLOUR GUIDE

Kudat

C.L. Chan

SABAH COLOUR GUIDE

KUDAT

Wendy Hutton

Foreword by

Y.A.B. Datuk Chong Kah Kiat, J.P.

Photographs by

C.L. Chan

Mike Cadman, Ben Chai, Wendy Hutton,
Tham Yau Kong, Tee Kim Ling, Lee Yen Phin,
W.M. Poon, Poong Foo On and Sydney Wee

Natural History Publications (Borneo)
Kota Kinabalu
2003

Published by

NATURAL HISTORY PUBLICATIONS (BORNEO) SDN. BHD.
(Company No. 216807-X)
A913, 9th Floor, Phase 1, Wisma Merdeka
P.O. Box 15566
88864 Kota Kinabalu, Sabah, Malaysia
Tel: 088-233098 Fax: 088-240768
e-mail: chewlun@tm.net.my
Website: www.nhpborneo.com

Sabah Colour Guide: Kudat by Wendy Hutton

ISBN 983-812-073-1

First published 18 March 2003.

Printed in Malaysia.

Contents

C.L. Chan

Foreword

by

Y.A.B. Datuk Chong Kah Kiat, J.P.
Chief Minister
and
Minister of Tourism, Environment, Science and Technology, Sabah

Kudat, like other well-established localities in Sabah, Land Below The Wind, offers many aspects that can be directly enjoyed by the visitor without any trouble. Still, it is always the special flavour of a destination that creates its own special draw. In Kudat, this springs to the fore—unadulterated original townlife with a vast Bornean hinterland; a mixture of various cultures that welcomes visitors; wild, windy shores; pampering amidst natural settings. This is the tourist's own corner of Borneo that will either start you off fresh on your sojourns in a special land, or help you wind down to recapture all the special moments that have been savoured.

It is my hope that this Guidebook will be a useful introduction to Kudat's special nature, as well as a worthy companion to enjoying Kudat. To our visitors and friends, therefore, we bid you "Selamat Datang" to this most fascinating ambience that is Kudat.

Chong Kah Kiat, J.P.
7th February 2003

Ben Chai

Introduction

Tranquil, beautiful and only starting to be discovered by local and foreign visitors alike, Kudat district is home to Sabah's most traditional tribal group, the Rungus. fascinating and friendly people, many of them still follow traditional lifestyles and produce some of Sabah's finest handicrafts. This unique tribe of soft-spoken people live in a district renowned for its glorious white-sandy beaches, while in a modern context, there is good and inexpensive seafood, recreational facilities including an 18-hole golf course and plentiful accommodation.

C.L. Chan

C.L. Chan

The people of Kudat, in the unspoilt northwestern corner of Sabah, are remarkably warm and welcoming.

Kudat is renowned for endless beautiful beaches washed by the South China Sea.

After the region was briefly the focus of attention during the first-ever British settlement in Southeast Asia (an abortive attempt to found a trading post on Balambangan island north of Kudat), and after operating as the capital of British North Borneo from 1882 until 1884, Kudat slipped from the history books, going about its existence with little attention from the outside.

The major reason for this was its isolation. Given the rugged nature of northern Borneo's terrain, Kudat was accessible primarily by boat until a road was begun in the 1960s, linking Sikuati (just 20 km west of Kudat town) with Kota Belud and on to Kota Kinabalu. Today, with the completion of a highway between Kota Kinabalu and Kota Belud and the upgrading of the road on to Kudat, the town is now only 175 km and about two-and-a-half hours from Sabah's capital.

Until a recent surge in development and infrastructure, the district moved along quietly and uneventfully, concentrating largely on the coconut and seafood industries. Increasing tourism in Sabah encouraged a limited number of visitors to traditional Rungus communities and longhouses from the early 1990s. As tourism has gained pace, a network of homestays has been established in Kudat district, offering an opportunity for visitors to experience a range of activities. In addition, several new hotels and a couple of resorts (one in Kudat and another near a popular beach), and the extension of the existing 9-hole golf course to a full 18 holes, have all increased Kudat's appeal.

C.L. Chan

C.L. Chan

C.L. Chan

Nowhere in Kudat is far from the sea. The northern end of Borneo, the world's third largest island, is deeply indented by Marudu Bay, with Kudat peninsula to the west and Bengkoka peninsula to the east looking rather like a couple of animal ears from the air. The Kudat region consists of gently rolling hills, many of them covered with coconut plantations, with increasing amounts of oil palm to the south and remnants of forest plantations, mostly planted in the 1980s. Kudat town is located on a peninsula which forms one end of a small bay tucked into the western side of Marudu Bay.

Beautiful beaches line the west coast of the Kudat peninsula, leading up to Simpang Mengayau. This dramatic headland, the northwestern tip of all of Borneo, looks over the South China Sea and the lighthouse on Pulau Kalampunian, with a glorious sweep of beach to the west and shallower tidal beaches running down the eastern side of the peninsula almost to Kudat town itself. Located due north of Kudat is the flat, virtually deserted island of Balambangan, while to the northeast is the larger and hilly Pulau Banggi.

Wendy Hutton

Pulau Balambangan (opposite, above) and Pulau Kalampunian (opposite, below) lie north of the Borneo mainland. Workers husking coconuts (above); this important crop is the star of the annual Coconut Festival held in Kudat.

Coutesy of Dr Heng Aik Cheng

DELt M. & N. HANHART LITH. PRINTERS

ILLANOAN PIRATE

(TAMPASSOOK, BORNEO)

In The Beginning

It is not certain just how many centuries the Rungus, a sub-group of the Kadazandusun ethnic group, have been in the Kudat district. They traditionally lived inland in longhouse communities, safe from pirates who frequented the coast.

In 1752, a British fleet took temporary control of Manila from the colonial Spanish, and released the imprisoned Sultan of Sulu. In gratitude, he gave the British control of part of the northern coast of Borneo, together with Banggi and Balambangan islands. Alexander Dalrymple, an Englishman who had visited Balambangan, conceived the idea of developing the island as a staging post for Britain's developing trade with China. However, the East India Company refused to meet Dalrymple's demands for total control over the settlement, as well as a commission on all cargo, so John Herbert was appointed chief of Britain's first Southeast Asian trading post.

Herbert landed in Balambangan with a couple of vessels in December 1773, building military barracks, a stockade, housing and warehouses. Unfortunately for the East India Company, they chose the wrong man, as Herbert embezzled large sums of money and goods. Furthermore, he mistreated the Suluks who settled there, and eventually they rebelled, raiding the settlement in 1775, burning it to the ground and making off with cannons, muskets, gold bars, Spanish silver dollars and a huge quantity of goods. Balambangan was reoccupied in 1803 but failed to prosper and was abandoned for the second time in 1805.

Attention turned briefly to Pulau Banggi in 1865, when the Sultan of Brunei leased it to the American consul, Charles Lee Moses, for 10 years. Although it was used as a depot for the American navy, there were no attempts to establish a permanent settlement.

The discovery of oil by Franz Witti (an explorer hired by the British North Borneo Chartered Company) in the region known as Kampung

---

Piracy was a problem during the 18th and 19th centuries; the graves of the family of Tun Mustapha (overleaf) are found at Limau Limauan.

M.C. Cadman

Minyak (26 km from Kudat town) was perhaps one of the reasons why the Company chose Kudat as the site for their first settlement.

A group of British landed in the area near the present location of Kudat town in December 1881, together with some Brunei Malays, and began clearing the land. The following year, the British North Borneo Chartered Company (which had bought rights to Sabah from the Sultans of Brunei and Sulu) officially established Kudat as the headquarters of their new settlement, which they named British North Borneo. However, Kudat remained the capital for only two years, when water shortages forced the administration to move to Sandakan.

When the British first arrived, the Chief of the Rungus community was Temenggong Kurantud. Datu Harun (father of the late Tun Mustapha Harun, who became a Chief Minister of Sabah) represented the Muslim community, most of them descendants of Bajau, Illanun and Suluks originally from the southern Philippines. These two leaders signed an agreement of cooperation with the British representatives of the Chartered Company, who promised to bring development and prosperity to the region.

The British soon made their new settlement a pleasant place. A visitor in 1886 fell for the quiet charms of Kudat, remarking that "its situation is far prettier than that of Elopura. It is neater and cleaner and the bungalows have walls of wood… There is a splendid beach extending for miles, and wonderful to relate, we actually found some attempts at gardening."

New Arrivals

When the British set up the British North Borneo Company, the population of Sabah was estimated to be around 150,000, although some historians believe it may have been as few as 60,000. The small Rungus population of Kudat was insufficient to provide a compliant workforce for the British, who had bought Sabah from remote

Courtesy of Sabah Museum

Hakka immigrants (above and overleaf) helped create flourishing coconut farms out of the jungle. Hakka women, in their distinctive hats, were renowned as hard-working labourers both in Kudat and other areas of the state.

sultans whose control was largely nominal, and who had never bothered to consult the locals before giving away control over their land. In order to develop their new possession, the Chartered Company needed labourers and therefore arranged for the import of Chinese workers.

Courtesy of Sabah Museum

The earliest groups of Chinese arrivals to Kudat and Sandakan did not undergo any selection process and proved unsuited to developing the land. For example, it was estimated that 222 of the 348 Chinese living in Kudat town were shopkeepers, most of whom had been in Hong Kong. What the new settlement needed was agriculturists, not shopkeepers and traders. A pioneer of the Basel Missionary Society to China was engaged to bring families of Christian Hakkas to settle in Kudat. Known for their skill as agriculturists and their devotion to land rather than to trade or commerce, the Hakkas proved to be an ideal choice.

The first small group arrived in January 1883, with a second group of 14 families (96 people altogether) arriving three months later. Another 27 families followed in 1886, all these pioneers settling in Lau San area, about 6 km out of town. Yet another group of Hakka settlers arrived in 1889, establishing themselves in a new settlement, Sinsanba. As new arrivals continued to come, they moved further away from the town to Pinangsoo, Tamalang and eventually as far as Sikuati.

These early Hakka settlers were offered generous terms by the Chartered Company, including free land and tools, and were given food rations for the first six months. They were required to cultivate half their 10-acre plot (which they had to wrest from the primary jungle) with rice and other cash

Lee Yen Phin

The Basel Church at Lau San.

Ben Chai

Chinese immigrants not only established farms but were involved in trading, like this shopkeeper in Mattungong Lama (above).

crops, while the remainder could be used for subsistence crops. The government also granted the Basel Mission land for churches, schools and cemeteries, and the Hakkas almost immediately set up informal schools teaching in Chinese. In addition, they were involved in the founding of the Catholic St Peter's School in Kudat in 1890, then set up the Lok Yuk Primary School in Kudat the same year.

The first Hakka migrants were joined by others over the next three to four decades, as well as by Chinese from the Hokkien, Cantonese and

Teochew dialect groups. The Hakkas set about transforming the landscape of Kudat, establishing the coconut plantations which are still the dominant feature of much of today's landscape. (The total area under coconut cultivation in the district is currently around 5,740 hectares, with over 3,000 families involved in coconut farming, including more than 600 on Banggi.)

Rubber also became an important crop, especially after a government guarantee in 1906 that there would be no tax on rubber exports for the next fifty years. Trial plantings were carried out in Lau San, and newer arrivals planted rubber around Pinangsoo, Bak Bak and Tamalang. However, rubber prices fluctuated considerably over the years, and today, rubber has been largely replaced by oil palm.

Owing to its relative inaccessibility, Kudat remained far from the active agricultural centres which grew up along the east coast, on the west coast around Kota Kinabalu and in the interior area around Tenom, which was linked by rail with Jesselton as early as 1905.

Tee Kim Ling

A traditional rice storage barn stands in front of a simple Rungus house.

C.L. Chan

The Rungus

Because of their isolation from the mainstream of development in Sabah until recently, the Rungus (a sub-group of the indigenous Kadazandusun) is Sabah's most traditional people. Actually divided into three separate linguistic sub-groups, the Rungus live on both sides of Marudu Bay, in the Kudat and Bengkoka peninsulas. Although sharing many of their beliefs, rituals and festivals with the rest of the Kadazandusun, the Rungus have a number of unique legends and practices, as well as distinctive costume and architecture.

Many Rungus work as agriculturists, wear a modified version of their traditional clothing and live in longhouses, although educated Rungus—like other Sabahans—can now be found in all walks of life. The women are renowned for their handicraft skills, particularly woven fabrics, beadwork and fine basketware.

C.L. Chan

Rungus girls decked out in their traditional finery, including stunning beaded necklaces and girdles, and wide brass armband.

C.L. Chan

C.L. Chan

Ben Chai

W.M. Poon

Although Rungus women now wear modern dress such as long pants or sarongs with t-shirts for daily work (above left), their traditional finery (above, top) is perhaps the most striking in all of Sabah. Rungus women are renowned for their handicraft, including fine basketware (above), but also turn their hand to more prosaic items such as brooms made from coconut husks (left).

Traditional ways of life are changing, and the majority of Rungus now choose to live in individual family dwellings rather than longhouses. A large number have converted to Christianity, while some have become Muslim.

Unlike the longhouses of Sarawak, the traditional Rungus longhouse does not contain a large number of unrelated families living under one roof. Rather, it starts as a single family dwelling and as the daughters marry, a new house is built for them and their husbands alongside the parents' house. And so the longhouse grows over the generations, sometimes augmented by more distant family members who ask for permission

Typical folded men's head gear (above); brass coil armbands are now worn only by older women (opposite).

Tham Yau Kong

Wendy Hutton

to join the longhouse. Villages sometimes consist of two or three longhouses, plus a few single family dwellings, with one headman for the whole village.

Longhouses were once built solely of locally available materials such as timber, thatch, bamboo and large slabs of bark. They are slightly raised above the ground on stilts, with a communal gallery running the length of the building. Private family quarters, consisting of a main room with a cooking area at the rear, are located on one side of the gallery. At the other edge is a deep raised platform, usually floored with split bamboo, allowing plenty of air to circulate. The outer wall of the longhouse gallery, which slopes outward from the base up to the extending roof, is made of

Why Rungus Women Wear Brass Coils

There is a charming legend explaining why Rungus women traditionally wore cumbersome brass coils wrapped around their lower legs and wrists, the latter coils held in place by white shell bangles. According to the story, a Rungus man saw a group of mermaids come ashore, remove their tails and play happily on the sand. Watching them from behind a rock, he fell in love with one of the mermaids. He stole her tail and buried it in the sand so she could not return to the sea with her friends, then took her home and married her. To prevent her from running back to the sea, he not only refused to reveal where he had hidden her tail but encircled her legs and wrists with heavy brass coils so their weight would prevent her from swimming away from him.

evenly spaced poles, once again ensuring that the breeze is allowed to circulate.

This platform is where much of the daily life and evening activities take place, where children play, women weave or make brooms, dogs sleep or scrap and men solve the problems of the world. It is also where unmarried men and male visitors to the longhouse sleep at night; women visitors are invited to sleep inside the family room.

Rungus women's weaving skills are legendary. Home-grown cotton is coloured black with plant dye, spun to make thread and then hand-woven into fabric on a back-strap loom. This is used as a mid-length wrap-around skirt by the women, or sewn into wide-legged trousers for the men, who add a colourfully embroidered headcloth or *sigal*, often worn whenever venturing out (even just for a day's work in the fields), and during festive occasions.

Skilled at needle-weaving, Rungus women sometimes make intricate panels to form a narrow colourful band set into their black skirts. The finest weavers also work traditional motifs into the fabric used for men's jackets (which can cost as much as RM700). Turning their skills to more marketable items, many Rungus women now weave narrow colourful sashes for sale to visitors, sometimes with the name of the longhouse woven in or, on request, the name of the buyer.

Wendy Hutton

For centuries, imported beads have been a treasured item throughout Borneo, and today, antique beads are worth an enormous sum of money. Strings of beads form an integral part of a Rungus woman's outfit, worn as necklaces, slung around the hips and criss-crossed over the chest. A large flat white disk of shell, pierced in the centre, is also worn around the throat.

Another product of Rungus weaving skills is seen in the beaded necklaces, bracelets, sashes and other items fashioned out of tiny modern glass or plastic beads, which are worn by women who do not possess heirloom beads and are also offered for sale.

Tee Kim Ling

Older Rungus men rarely go out without their sigal *or folded head cloth (above). Traditional brass arm coils are so difficult to put on that the women very rarely remove them (opposite). Brass anklets have almost disappeared today.*

Some of the finest basketware in Sabah is made by Rungus women, using material from a wild twining fern known as *lingkong*. This is tightly coiled and fashioned into attractive trays, plates, bowls, lidded boxes and other useful items. Although traditionally left to reveal their natural straw-like colour, many of the basketware items now have brightly coloured threads woven in.

A more prosaic item made by the hard-working Rungus women is simple brooms of coconut husk fibre, which are sold in local markets. (In the village of Terongkongan Laut, the road is often covered with split coconut husks, left there for passing cars to do the initial work of crushing them flat.)

C.L. Chan

Kudat Town

Kudat is considered by some as the most attractive town in all of Sabah, and the embodiment of the aphorism "small is beautiful". Apart from its ideal location by the sea, it is spacious, clean and orderly, with plenty of trees, flowering shrubs and open spaces. Until about 25 years ago, Kudat town consisted of little more than one major road and a few side streets lined with two-storey shophouses. Residents lived in timber houses scattered around the town or in the stilt village (Kampung Air) tucked into the tiny inlet at the foot of the town. There were the usual schools, churches, mosques and temples, as well as government administrative buildings, a Rest House for visiting officials and a *padang* or green where sports were played adjoining the Kudat Town Board. The harbour was frequented by local fishing boats and occasional coastal steamers, but apart from that, Kudat saw little activity.

W.M. Poon

Kudat town began around an inlet (above) tucked into Kudat Bay.

MAP OF KUDAT TOWN
(Not to scale)
Jalan Marudu (to Kota Kinabalu)
Jalan Abdul Rahim
Kudat Rest House
Kudat CBR Building
KWSP (EPF Building)
Basketball Court
Night Market
Community Centre
Car Park
Mosque
Jalan Dato
Shell Station
Petrol Station (Shell)
Tennis Court
Car Park
JPPS/ Jabatan Laut
Jalan OKK Hj Ghani
Hokken Association
Chinese Temple
Post Office
Hotel Ria
Padang (Field)
Jalan Abdul Rahim
Jalan Lo Thien Chok
Malaysia Day Memorial
Jalan Wan Siak
Police Quarters
Kedai Telecom
Police Station
Pertubuhan Perladang
Merak Hati Sdn Bhd
Jalan Hor
Car Park
Jalan Lo Thien Chok
Hotel Sunrise
Bus Terminal
Public Toilet
Jalan Pasar Am
Carpark
Jalan Melati
Yayasan Sabah
Carpark
Pelabuhan dan Permaga
Petrol Station (Esso)
Kudat Ferry Terminal
Clothes Market
Market
Jalan Kemboja
Immigration Department
Fishing Harbour
Public Toilet
Kudat Port
Jalan Melor
Vegetable & Fruit Market
Maybank Berhad
Jalan Cempaka
Customs Building
Car Park
KFC
Hotel Dream Garden
Milimewa Supermarket
Hotel Kinabalu
Jalan Melor
Bank Simpanan Nasional
Upper Deck Hotel
Grace Garden Hotel
Hotel Kian Da
Jalan Lintas
Kudat Fish Market
Food Stalls (Seaview)
Ko-Nelayan Building

Kudat Town

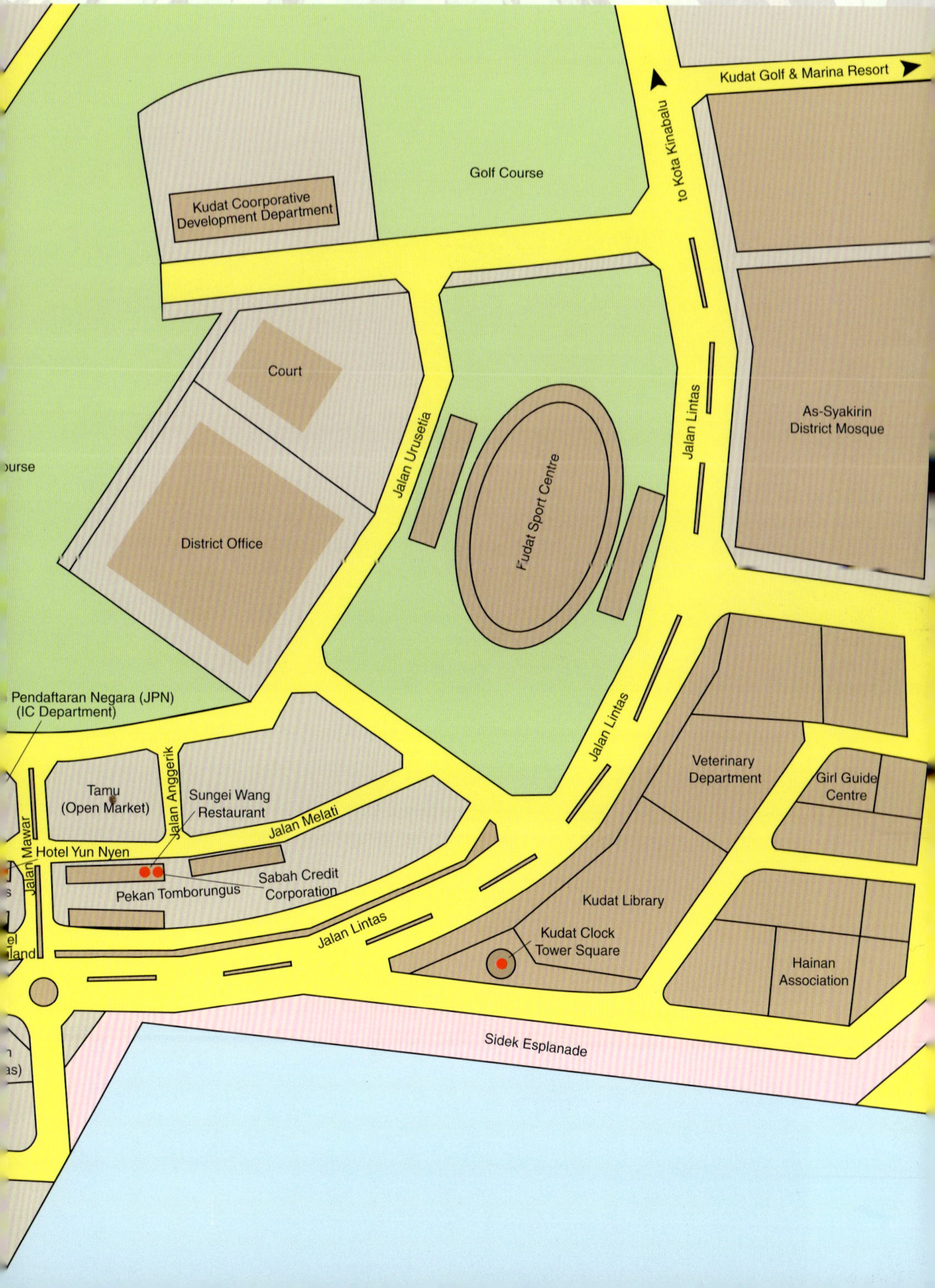

Kudat Golf & Marina Resort
to Kota Kinabalu
Golf Course
Kudat Coorporative Development Department
Court
District Office
Jalan Urusetia
Kudat Sport Centre
Jalan Lintas
As-Syakirin District Mosque
Pendaftaran Negara (JPN) (IC Department)
Tamu (Open Market)
Jalan Anggerik
Sungei Wang Restaurant
Jalan Melati
Jalan Mawar
Hotel Yun Nyen
Sabah Credit Corporation
Pekan Tomborungus
Veterinary Department
Girl Guide Centre
Kudat Library
Kudat Clock Tower Square
Hainan Association
Sidek Esplanade

C.L. Chan

C.L. Chan

C.L. Chan

C.L. Chan

W.M. Poon

Large-scale reclamation has enabled the town of Kudat to spread on both sides of the peninsula. The Rest House (top right) and marine fish ponds (centre right) are among the many new structures in Kudat.

Poong Foo On

Named in honour of Datuk Sidek Danta (above centre) and officially launched by Datuk Chong Kah Kiat, Chief Minister of Sabah (above left), Sidek Esplanade has become a popular place to relax by the bay.

C.L. Chan

How Kudat Got Its Name

The peninsula on the northern side of the small bay set into the western side of Marudu Bay was known to the Rungus as Tambun, which means peninsula in their dialect. This land, where the British decided to establish their settlement, had been used for generations as a trading ground for Brunei traders, who exchanged gongs, ironware, Chinese ceramics and clothing for the jungle produce, rice and corn offered by the Rungus. The Rungus called this trading area Tanjung Berungus or Tomburungan, after the Tomborungus River that ran into the inlet where the stilt houses of Kampung Air still exist (the river has since disappeared). It is said that when the British first arrived and asked for the name of the place, the Rungus mistakenly thought they wanted to identify the coarse grass or *lalang* growing there, so said *kutad* (*lalang* in Rungus dialect). Eventually, the name was corrupted to Kudat, and was used in preference to the old name of Tomborungus.

Tee Kim Ling

New coffee-shops in Kudat retain their old-world charm through the use of antique marble-topped tables and chairs.

C.L. Chan

C.L. Chan

C.L. Chan

The new Kudat Sport Centre was first used for the 2002 Merdeka Day celebrations.

Kudat's isolation was diminished somewhat by the building of a road to Kota Belud in the 1960s, but the journey to Kota Kinabalu took around 4 hours. Another step forward in the same decade was the development of Kudat's 9-hole golf course on the land next to the Town Board.

Despite its isolation from the mainstream of British North Borneo, Kudat produced a number of prominent politicians over the years. Lo Thien Chok, a leading Hakka trader whose name is remembered in the main road of Kudat, was the Chinese representative in the state Legislative Council from 1914 to 1926. Mustapha Harun (later to become Tun Mustapha) and Haji Sidek Danta co-founded the USNO political party in 1961, two years prior to Sabah gaining independence within Malaysia. Tun Mustapha was the first Governor of Sabah after the formation of Malaysia, and went on to become Sabah's third Chief Minister in 1967, a post he held until 1976.

A leading Rungus politician, Datuk Idrus Matakim, was the State Assemblyman for the Langkon district from 1967 until 1976, as well as an Assistant Minister of Agriculture and Fisheries and Minister of Culture, Youth and Sports. He was also actively involved in the opening of several schools, the Kudat Youth Hall and establishing a fisherman's cooperative.

C.L. Chan

Kudat Golf Club clubhouse (above); the 18-hole course is adjacent to a harbour-side golf and marina resort.

Poong Foo On

C.L. Chan

C.L. Chan

C.L. Chan

C.L. Chan

C.L. Chan

Ben Chai

C.L. Chan

The Upper Deck hotel (opposite) offers views over Kudat bay. Some of Kudat's Chinese community worship in the ornate temple in the heart of town, and observe traditional religious festivals.

Tee Kim Ling

The shape of Kudat was dramatically altered in the 1970s, when a massive project costing close to RM100 million reclaimed 500 acres from the sea, including an area designed for use as a marina. Blocks of 3-storey shophouses with spacious pedestrian-only walkways between them were built on part of the reclaimed land to make a new shopping centre in the early 1980s. A large open area between this and the edge of the golf course was designated as the open market or *tamu* ground. This new part of Kudat town was called Pekan Tomborungus, after the original name for Kudat.

Kudat is famed for its excellent and inexpensive seafood and locally grown peanuts.

Tee Kim Ling

Datuk Chong Kah Kiat, one of Sabah's most illustrious sons and the Chief Minister from 2001 to 2003, was Kudat State Assemblyman from 1981 to 1985 and again since 1999. Through his interest and determination, Kudat has transformed into being more accessible to the world, while retaining its own special charms.

One of the most striking new features is the Sidek Esplanade, running along the bay on the edge of the reclaimed land. Spacious, clean and evenly surfaced, the attractive esplanade has plenty of seating, picnic shelters, adequate play areas for children, plenty of room for jogging or strolling, and several food stalls. The Sidek Esplanade has become enormously popular with locals who relax in the sea breezes, especially in the late afternoon and early evening, when pulsating coloured lights transform artificial coconut palms and fanciful "trees" into a fairyland.

Also built on reclaimed land adjacent to part of the golf course is a 17-acre track and field Sport Centre, where the State Merdeka Day celebrations were held in 2002. The Kudat Golf Club was able to extend its course by another 9 holes in 2002, utilising some of the reclaimed land opposite its clubhouse. A new three-star resort has been built adjacent to the golf course overlooking the area originally planned as a marina. Other buildings on this reclaimed land include a private shipyard and fisheries export company, Kudat Library, the Kudat District Mosque, the Kudat Girl Guides Association Headquarters and a number of commercial buildings.

"Old Kudat" is still focused around Jalan Lo Thien Chok, where traditional fan-cooled coffee shops, mixed traders and provision shops are now joined by a few cybercafes and the occasional boutique. The opening in 2002 of Kudat's first air-conditioned supermarket, with a department store on the first floor and a hotel on the third level, has brought a touch of modernity

C.L. Chan

to this part of town. A new 6-storey hotel sits next to the large and colourful Fook Tek Ser Chinese temple which dominates Jalan Marudu. This temple, the old mosque at the main roundabout opposite a petrol station and the churches on the hills nearby bear witness to the religious diversity of Kudat.

The wooden houses of Kampung Air still perch on stilts over the inlet where the Tomborungus river once flowed into the sea. Nearby, Kudat's fishing fleet comes in with their catch, much of it exported or sent south to Kota Kinabalu. It is worth a stroll around this area and towards the jetty, where daily ferries leave for Pulau Banggi. Simple privately owned wooden boats, sometimes with families living aboard, jostle with the commercial fishing fleet, which makes an important contribution to the local economy (one company exports prawns, squid, lobsters and some live fish to Hong Kong, Japan, Taiwan and the UK).

The Kudat Fish Market, opposite the two-storey General Market, is known for its inexpensive seafood, although those with connections buy directly from the fishing boats before the choicest seafood disappears. The main market offers a range of foodstuffs, groceries, poultry and meat on the ground floor, including the famous local moist coconut candy (*kuih kelapa*) sold by several Chinese vendors specialising in local cakes, biscuits and snacks. Inexpensive cooked food is sold on the first level of the market, which is particularly busy for breakfast.

One of the most interesting areas of the market, however, is the grassy spot under the trees between the back of the market and the car park. This is an unofficial Rungus meeting area, where older men wearing the traditional folded headgear squat over sets of gongs, often playing them to encourage buyers (or, perhaps, to pass the time of day). Some of the women sell herbal medicines or a few old brassware objects, while others — the older women often wearing the traditional brass and shell bracelets, strings of antique beads and homespun sarongs — seem to be just taking in the scene.

Between the main market and the road, a single-storey building is home to the fruit and vegetable market, worth checking out for some unusual produce including wild jungle vegetables and fruits. A couple of stalls at the back, nearest the fish market, specialise in shells and shell ornaments, while at one side of the building, it is sometimes possible to buy fresh edible seaweed, oysters and other shellfish.

Not far from the main market, the *tamu* ground at Pekan Tomborungus (which has a stage for cultural performances during festivals such as the Coconut Festival or Pesta Kelapa each September) becomes a scene of lively activity late every Tuesday afternoon and on into the evening, when the Pasar Malam or Night Market is held.

W.M. Poon

Although the large, relatively new Kudat District Mosque (opposite) is located opposite the Kudat Sports complex, this older mosque (above) at the main roundabout still attracts many worshippers.

KUDAT PENINSULA

Exploring Kudat District

VISITING THE BEACHES

The west coast of the Kudat peninsula has some of the finest beaches in Sabah, particularly those stretching from Teringkai on up to Tanjung Simpang Mengayau, the northern tip. The beaches along the eastern side of the peninsula as far south as Kudat town tend to be shallow and rocky, although there is one fine beach and a popular seaside picnic area close to town. Further south in Marudu Bay, the coast is often swampy with mangroves, with only the occasional strip of sand. A network of roads, often unsealed but still navigable without a 4-wheel drive, criss-crosses the peninsula, inviting exploration of the small settlements and longhouses en route to many of the beaches. Most roads are also ideal for mountain biking.

C.L. Chan

Bak Bak picnic area is close to the town, but the beach (above) cannot compare with those further afield.

C.L. Chan

C.L. Chan

C.L. C

C.L. Chan

C.L. Chan

C.L. Chan

An aerial shot of Simpang Mengayau, the northern tip of Borneo (previous pages) shows its dramatic beauty. Closer inspection reveals sandstone rocks carved by the wind and waves. Pantai Kalampunian, just before Simpang Mengayau, is one of the finest beaches in all of Sabah, with crystal clear waters and gently sloping sand.

The closest beach to Kudat is **Pantai Bak Bak**. Just 5 km out of town is a clearly marked junction, the right fork (Jalan Sin San) leading on to a junction with Jalan Pinangsoo 2.7 km away. The road on the right at this junction leads to Bak Bak, just 1.6 km away. A long grassy strip with a number of large shady trees stretches above a rather rocky beach, good for swimming only at high tide. However, picnic shelters, tables, a few barbecue areas (bring your own grill), a changing block and food stalls operating on Sundays make Bak Bak very popular for a relaxing day by the seaside.

Continuing on from Pantai Bak Bak for almost 4 km, the road comes to a fork. Take the right hand fork (a sealed road) for 400 metres through a mangrove swamp and the reward is the aptly named White Sandy Beach, or **Pasir Putih**. Although just south of the small village of Kampung Tajau Laut, this fine beach is generally deserted. The soft white sand is gently sloping, making this spot good for swimming whatever the state of the tide.

To reach **Pantai Kalampunian** (one of the finest beaches in the Kudat peninsula) and the headland of **Simpang Mengayau**, take Jalan Sin San 5 km out of Kudat. Instead of turning right towards Bak Bak, continue straight ahead on Jalan Pinangsoo. This road leads through endless coconut groves and past atmospheric old 2-storey wooden farmhouses, the coconut plantations created out of the jungles cleared by the first Hakka settlers to this

C.L. Chan

Countless bays and beaches await adventurous travellers.

C.L. Chan

Sunjamal Resort (above) is near popular Pantai Kelambu (opposite).

region over a century ago. Around 16 km beyond the Bak Bak junction, the road arrives at a sign-posted junction on the left to Marang Parang.

Take Jalan Marang Parang until the start of the village, just 1.4 km from the Jalan Tiga Papan junction. A narrow dirt road to the right, marked Jalan Kalampunian,(and with a sign post courtesy of a local resort) leads to a long curving bay with stunning soft white sand and strikingly clear water. This is perhaps the finest swimming beach in all of Kudat, but as it faces west, the afternoon sun can be hot and there are few shady trees.

Continuing on past the police security post at the north of the beach, the road comes to a fork. The right-hand fork leads to a small, rather shallow beach on the eastern side of the headland, with plenty of shady spots for relaxing, while the road straight ahead leads up to Tanjung Simpang Mengayau, the northwestern tip not only of Sabah but of the whole island of Borneo. Known to the colonial British as "The Parting of the Pirate Ways" (for this area was once rife with piracy), Simpang Mengayau translates more correctly as lingering or loitering crossroads. And the superb views from this vantage point do indeed encourage lingering. The dramatic beauty of the headland—with spectacular and seemingly endless vistas—is accentuated by the swirling patterns etched into the cliffs, sculpted by aeons of wind and pounding waves.

Nature has obligingly carved steps into the headland, making it easy to clamber down to the flat rocky shelves surrounded by sea. On a calm day, this is an excellent spot to snorkel, with fine, undamaged hard corals and a number of small colourful fish. Enthusiastic fishermen can sometimes be seen trying their luck in this area.

Another popular beach is not far away. Instead of turning right into Jalan Kalampunian at Kampung Marang Parang, continue straight ahead. It is only another 2 km to a small sealed road off to the right, leading to **Pantai Kelambu** just 1.5 km further away. (Half-way between Kampung Marang Parang and the Pantai Kelambu junction, the attractive **Sunjamal Resort** can be seen nestling on the hillside to the left.)

Pantai Kelambu is in a spectacular location, a tiny peninsula with large sweeping bays on either side creating two swimming beaches, so whatever the direction of the wind, there is always a calm area for swimming. A raised sand spit used to connect the mainland with the rocky hills of Pulau Kelambu, a dot of an island about 200 metres offshore. However, recent clearing of some trees to make a sealed parking and picnic area seems to have disturbed the currents and caused erosion of this sand spit. The picnic area is usually very busy on Sundays, but a short walk along the sand of either bay promises privacy.

(To reach Pantai Kelambu, Pantai Kelampunian and Simpang Mengayau without having to go through Kudat, take Jalan Tamalang, to the left 14 km before Kudat town. This road links up with Jalan Pinangsoo and on to Jalan Papan Tiga.)

C.L. Chan

A wide bay with a deep river on its northern side is known as **Pantai Kimihang**, after the nearby village. To reach this, take Jalan Bangau 16 km from Kudat (on the right of the main road if heading out of Kudat). Follow this road past coconut groves and occasional rice paddies (where there are often water buffalos and their attendant slender white egrets) for 5 km, ignoring the right-hand turn (Jalan Kimihang). The road ends at the edge of the long bay, although it is possible to follow a dirt track at the edge of the beach for a few hundred metres to the southern end of the bay.

A few houses and a barn-like church are located along the north of the bay, where a wide river merges with the sea by the hills. Although Kimihang beach is shallow, it is a good spot for picnicking and camping, with shady trees. Swimming can be fun at the river mouth (especially if it happens to be low tide), and local fishermen frequently try their luck with nets as the tide comes in.

The long white sandy beach of **Sikuati** is tricky to reach, and its exposed position means that only a few pandanus trees grow on the sand dune at the back of the beach; there can also be currents, making it dangerous for those who are not good swimmers. It is, however, a spectacular spot, and the locals swear that it is an excellent place to catch squid and prawns at night. Because a bridge leading to Kampung Andab, the easiest way to gain access to the beach, seems to be permanently broken, the best route to take is Jalan Radio Station, roughly 18 km before Kudat (the tall radio aerial on the left of the road can not be missed).

Jalan Radio Station soon forks; take the left fork and follow the road (taking care over innumerable speed bumps built near the houses) for 2.6 km, then turn right at Kampung Korina and drive for 0.8 km until reaching a gravel road on the right. Take this road and within 1 km, the road arrives at a very high wooden arch with a huge cartoon-style coloured figure. It is difficult to decide what this is meant to be until pens with dozens of ostriches come into view. This is, of course, an ostrich farm. The road leads another 0.5 km to the sand dunes, piled up by the action of the relentless South China Sea.

Spectacular cliffs are a feature of **Badarag**, with two tiny lagoons at the south end of Sikuati Beach. To reach these lagoons, drive along Jalan Sikuati Beach (24 km out of Kudat) and take the left fork which leads into a crowded fishing village. A scramble along the back of the lagoon to the right will bring you to the base of the cliffs, although it is probably easier to pay a local fisherman to paddle you there, or on to the stretch of sandy beach on the other side of the lagoon.

Further south, the beach of **Terongkongan** can be reached via Jalan Terongkongan, 26 km before Kudat. The road passes through Kampung Minyak (where there is a homestay programme). If you are interested in seeing the famous pools of oil, ask one of the villagers to guide you there for a small fee. Beyond Kampung Minyak, where the road forks, take the road to the left to Kampung Terongkongan, 6 km away. This road terminates at the coast, where a long sandy beach invites swimming.

Those in search of adventure should walk to the right (north) along Terongkongan beach for about 20 minutes to a small headland. Over the millennia, the sea has carved a narrow cave (known to the locals as **Gua Tindakop**) into the headland, allowing the sea to rush through. It is too

M.C. Cadman

Rocky foreshores reveal their treasures at low tide.

dangerous to try to enter the cave from the sea side unless it is low tide, but a clamber over the top of the headland will reveal a small sink hole (recognisable by the tree tops seen in a hollow). A short scramble down the sink hole leads to a sandy bottom, evidence of the sea reaching here through the cave at high tide. The locals tell tales of hidden treasure, or of Japanese hiding here during WWII, but given the small size of the cave, these would seem to be nothing more than tales. Nonetheless, it is exciting to stand at the back of the cave and watch the sea surging in.

A great panorama of rolling hills can be had from the road to **Bingolon**, to the right of the main road a couple of kilometres south of Parapat when heading out of Kudat. The road travels over rolling hills, past Bingolon (a small Rungus village) and ends 5.7 km away at Teluk Agal (sometimes called Teluk Tambularan), a deep narrow bay with the large river at its southern end. Although this is one of the most striking spots in the Kudat district, it is not necessarily private. A village of Cagayan fisherfolk, originally from the Philippines, is established here and the children are reluctant to let visitors explore or swim alone.

There is a long beach to the north of the small fishing village of **Indarasan Laut**, reached via the clearly marked junction on the main road for Kampung Tinangol, although this is shallow and not as attractive as Terongkongan.

C.L. Chan

Coconuts, once the mainstay of Kudat, still grow in large plantations where old-style wooden farmhouses can be seen.

Wendy Hutton

VISITING THE RUNGUS

There are dozens of isolated settlements, sometimes consisting of nothing more than a single longhouse, dotted all over the Kudat peninsula. Some of the more easily accessible villages just off the main road to Kudat town have become well known and are frequently visited. For those who enjoy travelling off the beaten track, however, there are still plenty of surprises tucked away in narrow valleys, on the hillsides or in the bays on either side of the peninsula.

Some 48 km south of Kudat town, **Mattungong** was once an important trading centre for Rungus living in this area. Although a regular weekly market or *tamu* is still held each Saturday at the side of the main road just before the old village — Pekan Lama Mattungong — the village itself is now virtually deserted, replaced by Pekan Baru Mattungong, further north and close to the villages of Gombizau and Sumangkap.

A visit to Pekan Lama Mattungong is a drive back in time. Less than 100 metres off the main Kudat road, a group of three unpainted wooden shops is all that remains of what was once the main shopping area. Wong Ban Siong,

Tee Kim Ling

C.L. Chan

C.L. Chan

Tham Yau Kong

While the markets are dominated by local women, shops are traditionally in the hands of Chinese traders.

who has traded here for the past fifty years, swings in his hammock on the wide verandah in front of his sundry shop-cum-home as he reminisces about the old days, when the quickest way to get to Kudat was to go by boat down the Mattungong river and up Marudu Bay.

One of the more active villages in the south, **Kampung Gombizau** (43 km out of Kudat) consists of a couple of longhouses and several private family dwellings, as well as a modest church. Advertised as the "Honey Bee Farm" (with a large sign at the turnoff on the main road), Gombizau's residents sell locally gathered honey. Enterprising headman, Mogawan Malis, was persuaded a few years ago to put several hives with honey bees near his longhouse. The surrounding woods provided plenty of nectar for the bees and the business flourished, encouraging other villagers to join in the activity. Visitors will be shown, on request, how the bees are smoked out of their hives and the honey gathered, and can buy pure honey for a very reasonable price.

Another interesting activity at Gombizau is the gathering of wild herbs, roots and other plant material to make traditional Rungus medicine based on recipes handed down over the generations by word of mouth. Known as *ubat seribu* or medicine of a thousand uses, this

Coconuts may still be a cash crop, but even sweeter rewards await villagers involved in honey production. Kg Gombizau welcomes visitors to see how the honey is produced and buy some as a tasty souvenir.

Tee Kim Ling

Tee Kim Ling

Tee Kim Ling

can be bought from the headman or his wife, Mangudizing, at the longhouse nearest the honey stall, or from in front of Kudat market (usually in the morning each Monday, Wednesday and Friday). It is claimed to help with high blood pressure, diabetes, infections and a host of other problems.

Less than 1 km further along the road towards Kudat is the clearly signposted village of **Sumangkap**, famous for its cottage industry of gong making. The longhouses of the old village have been replaced by individual family dwellings and simple workshops, with many of the houses showing an intriguing blend of traditional Rungus architecture along with modern styles and materials.

C.L. Chan

Gongs, either set horizontally in a frame or hung vertically, are the major Rungus musical instrument (although a nose flute is sometimes played by the older women). Richly embossed brass gongs made in Brunei, often with dragon motifs, were once an important trading item and these antiques fetch a very high price today.

Some 15 artisans (less than half the number working a decade ago) make gongs at Sumangkap, and are happy to demonstrate their skills (a nominal sum of RM3 is requested from visitors to the village). Sheets of thick aluminium alloy are cut and beaten to form gongs, often made to order with names or symbols embossed upon them.

C.L. Chan

Gong making is the main industry in Kg Sumangkap.

Sydney Wee

They vary in size from tiny souvenir gongs up to a giant of almost two metres across, hung outside the workshop of Darwin Kunama. A medium-sized gong will take two to three days to fashion, the final stages being a coat of dark anti-rust paint and a spray of matt gold paint on the raised centre. Although the gongs of Sumangkap lack the refinement of the gongs of bygone days, they still produce a pleasant tone.

Those who enjoy exploring off the beaten track could take Jalan Pinawantai, opposite the road leading to Kampung Gombizau. This road goes through the big settlement of Pinawantai and eventually passes the two huge longhouses of Kampung Nangka, on a hill to the left. Once roofed with *attap* thatch, these longhouses now have corrugated zinc roofs but are still striking. The road leads on to **Limau Limauan**, a settlement on a narrow peninsula jutting into Marudu Bay. The old Muslim cemetery on the headland, with its ornate marble gravestones where Tun Mustapha and some of his family are buried, bears witness to the existence of a village here for at least a century.

Tee Kim Ling

Longhouses built in traditional style but with modern bathing facilities, and homestays around Kg Minyak offer visitors the chance for a close-up look at Rungus life.

To complete a loop back to the main road (a round trip of about 42 km), drive via Ronggu, Lodung and Kumbatang, keeping an eye open for the occasional longhouse. The Rungus in this region are — like everywhere in Kudat — friendly and helpful. Even though some of the older women speak only Rungus, most of the younger generation speak Bahasa Malaysia, and one or two of the men may surprise you with their command of English.

Some 41 km south of Kudat (and clearly signposted), **Kampung Bavanggazo** is located in an attractive valley about 2.5 km from the main road. A purpose-built longhouse constructed entirely of traditional materials almost a decade ago was the first to offer visitors an insight into longhouse life (but with modern comforts such as showers and toilets). This longhouse was such a success that a second one was constructed opposite, with a small handicraft shop nearby. Run as a community project, the Bavanggazo longhouses can be

Tee Kim Ling

C.L. Chan

Tee Kim Ling

Tee Kim Ling

C.L. Chan

Tee Kim Ling

visited on a day trip, but for a better flavour of local life, including a meal of traditional food and an evening of dance and music, it is preferable to stay the night.

Another longhouse located about 500 metres before the original longhouses was expected to open at the end of 2002. This is operated by Maranjak, the man behind the establishment of the first tourism longhouses in Kampung Bavanggazo.

A homestay programme (known as Misompuru) centred around **Kampung Minyak**, 26 km south of Kudat, was begun in 2002. Around 35 families living in modern housing (with approved standards for bathing and toilet facilities) offer rooms to visitors interested in experiencing Rungus lifestyle. Many of the homes and surrounding gardens are attractive, and the welcome absolutely genuine. Visitors enjoy local food with their host family, and can even help gather the ingredients and preparing them if they wish. A wide range of activities and visits in the region are offered, depending upon the visitor's interests.

A trip over boardwalks above a mangrove swamp leads to the three small pools where oil seeps up from underground. Known to the Rungus for

---

Woven head cloths, sashes and beadwork can be bought from the women who created them in Kg Bavanggazo and Kg Tinangol. Gongs and old brassware can sometimes be found outside Kudat's main market.

Visitors learning new skills in Kg Bavanggazo longhouse.

Roasted corn is a popular snack enroute to Kudat.

generations and revered as a sacred site, these oil wells attracted the colonial British, but have never been exploited as they do not contain a commercially viable quantity of oil. It is nonetheless strange to see these oily pools backed by the dense mangroves.

A boat trip through the mangrove forest, swimming at nearby Terongkongan beach, exploring the cave in the headland, trekking to a small waterfall, gathering wild food, joining in cultural dances, fishing or visiting traditional longhouses and interesting villages near by are just some of the activities that can be arranged on the homestay programme.

Nothing remains of the atmospheric old wooden shophouses near the *tamu* area of **Sikuati**, which was once, along with Mattungong, one of the two most important trading centres of Kudat district. A completely new block of shophouses has been constructed, but the Sunday morning market or *tamu* is worth visiting, especially for the possibility of seeing Rungus items such as old beads, gongs and handwoven costumes, as well as for the lively atmosphere and some of the unusual fresh produce on sale.

PULAU BANGGI AND PULAU BALAMBANGAN

On a clear day, the high peak of Pulau Banggi and the distant flat sprawl of Pulau Balambangan sit tantalisingly on the horizon to the north. Kerakit, the main (but very small) settlement of **Pulau Banggi** is located at the island's southern tip and has schools, an informal food stall, a few simple shops, local government offices and a relatively new hospital; however, there is no tourism infrastructure at this stage. Scattered small settlements, including almost 50 fishing villages, dot the coast, with most of Banggi's inhabitants making a subsistence living from fishing and raising coconuts.

The original people of the island and of neighbouring Balambangan are Banggi, the smallest of Sabah's indigenous groups who have the distinction of speaking a non-Borneon language, thought to be related to one of the languages of Palawan in the southwestern Philippines. Today, the Banggi are rarely seen, living in isolated small groups.

Tee Kim Ling

Pulau Balambangan, site of an abortive 18th century British trading post, has only one small fishing village today. An important archaeological site is located in the far south of the island.

Kerakit (above) is the main centre on Pulau Banggi (above). A teardrop island (overleaf) lies amidst coral reefs between Banggi and the coast of Kudat.

Just south of Kerakit, the island of **Malleangan**—where a fine white sandy beach is backed with coconut palms with a few houses dotted about—is the sort of place which tempts the adventurous to camp and live the simple life for a few days.

Despite being chosen as the site of a British trading settlement in the 18th century, **Pulau Balambangan** today is virtually deserted, with just a small settlement, Kampung Batu Sireh, in the southeast. Flat, with an often-swampy coastline with coral reefs making approach by boat challenging, and with only brackish water, it is difficult to understand why the British would have chosen this in preference to Pulau Banggi as a site for a settlement.

Kampung Batu Sireh has given its name to a cave set in a limestone outcrop at one side of an exquisite tiny bay on the southern tip of

Balambangan. This is an important archaeological site, where evidence of human habitation some 16,000 years ago was uncovered. None of the remains are left on the site, but there is a splendid view from the cave mouth of the sea below. The waters of the bay invite swimming, although locals warn of estuarine crocodiles sometimes lurking in the vicinity.

North of Kampung Batu Sirih, at one side of a large and beautiful bay, Teluk Lung, the remnants of the abortive Balambangan settlement can still be uncovered in the scrub at the back of the beach. Shards of blue and white Chinese porcelain, broken terracotta tiles and glass melted by the heat of the fire which razed the settlement all bear silent witness to the past.

The clear clean waters of Teluk Lung are home to a research project aimed at studying the growth of different varieties of seaweed. This is in line with efforts to encourage seaweed farming to help improve the livelihood of fishermen in suitable coastal areas of Sabah. Long lines of several varieties of seaweed are buoyed in the water by plastic bottles, left to grow (provided the turtles do not help themselves to a free meal) until they can be dried and processed to carrageenan powder, exported for use in the food industry.

C.L. Chan

Practical Information

HOW TO REACH KUDAT

Air-conditioned buses leave Kota Kinabalu from near the Padang from around 7 am daily; the fare is RM10 one way (there are also less comfortable mini-buses plying the route). It is possible to share a long-distance taxi (RM 25 per person) or to charter it for RM100, between Kota Kinabalu and Kudat. In Kudat, buses leave from next to the Telekoms office, opposite the clothing market near Hotel Sunrise.

TOUR OPERATORS

Several tour operators based in Kota Kinabalu specialise in visits to the Kudat region.
Borneo Native Homestay arranges trips to the Misompuru Homestay at Kampung Minyak
Telephone: (0880) 717 458; (013) 897 2243; (016) 839 8998
Email: info@borneonativehomestay.com
Website: www.borneonativehomestay.com

TYK Adventure Tours Award-winning Tham Yau Kong offers budget-priced, personalised adventure and cultural travel in the Kudat region, taking visitors off the beaten track (often by mountain bike). Visitors can stay in comfort in Kudat or opt to spend the night in a longhouse.
Telephone: (088) 720 825; (018) 889 0709
Email: tykadto@tm.net.my

Nature Heritage Travel & Tours specialises in homestays around Sabah, including Misompuru at Kampung Minyak.
Telephone: (088) 318 747
Email: nhtt@nature-heritage.com
Website: www.nature-heritage.com

HOMESTAYS

Misompuru Homestay, Kampung Minyak
Co-ordinator: Jeffry Hayha
Telephone: (013) 872 1765; (016) 815 5056
Email: jyrcobra@hotmail.com
Website: www.sabah-homestay.com
Visitors stay in private Rungus homes approved as part of the homestay network, eating meals with their host family and arranging for whatever activities interest them.

Bavanggazo Longhouse, near Kampung Tinangol
Contact: Agnes or Adrian
Telephone: (088) 621 971
A total of 18 rooms in 2 traditional longhouses, plus 3 separate single/double chalets; modern shower and toilet facilities. Rates vary depending upon the number of guests, with reductions for groups of 11 or more. For 2 days/1 night, inclusive of welcome drink, dinner, cultural dances and breakfast, the cost is RM65 per person. Day trips inclusive of welcome drink, handicraft item and cultural dance for RM35 per person.

Wendy Hutton

TRANSPORT AROUND KUDAT

Local taxis operate around Kudat and surrounding regions, while there is also a long-distance ("out-station") taxi service to Kota Kinabalu. Taxis can be found opposite the Hotel Ria in Jalan Marudu, in front of Hotel Sunrise at the corner of Jalan Lo Thien Chok and in front of the market. It is possible to negotiate an hourly or daily rate for travel around Kudat district.

Boat Travel

An air-conditioned express boat departs daily from the Kudat jetty for Kerakit, on Pulau Banggi, at 9 am. At present, there is no organised charter service for fishing trips or exploration by boat. However, it is possible to negotiate directly with boat owners who can be found in the harbour (expect to pay around RM300 per day). Private boats frequently cross Marudu Bay to Telaga and other *kampungs* on the Bengkoka peninsula; there are plans to introduce a regular ferry service in the near future.

ACCOMMODATION

Hotel Greenland

Pekan Tomborungus
Telephone: (088) 613 211
One of several older 2-storey hotels located above the shops of Pekan Tomborungus. Basic but clean rooms with air-con, TV and attached bathrooms. RM49 (S); RM56 (D); Economy room with share bathroom RM35.

Kudat Golf & Marina Resort

Jalan Abdul Rahim (opposite Kudat Golf Club clubhouse)
Telephone: (088) 611 211
Opened in 2002, this attractive 3-star resort overlooks the second 9 holes of the golf course, and the waters of Marudu Bay. A total of 88 rooms and suites, coffee shop/restaurant, large swimming pool and children's wading pool. All rooms have air-con, TV, IDD telephone, mini-bar, coffee/tea making facilities. From RM180 (S/D) to RM330 for a sea-facing executive suite.

Poong Foo On

C.L. Chan

Kudat Rest House
Jalan Abdul Rahim (adjacent to the Padang, opposite the Lembaga Bandaran Kudat)
Telephone: (088) 622 708
The old government-run rest house was demolished in 2002 and replaced by a new, privately operated rest house in a quiet location overlooking the Kudat golf course. All rooms and suites are comfortably furnished with air-con, TV, private bathroom and balcony. Restaurant and outside dining area. RM80 (S/D); RM200 VIP Suite.

C.L. Chan

Ria Hotel
Jalan Marudu
Telephone: (088) 622 794
Six-storey hotel in central location opened in 2002, with 24 well-furnished rooms with air-con, TV, IDD telephone, mini-bar, coffee/tea making facilities; suites and deluxe rooms have a kitchenette. Conference facilities for up to 250. From RM88 (S/D) up to RM268.

Lee Yen Phin

Sunjamal Resort
Jalan Marang Parang
Telephone: (088) 622 455
E-mail: info@sunjamal.com
Website: www.sunjamal.com
An exclusive small resort in a landscaped hillside setting, with a view over the sea from its restaurant, Sunjamal offers the ultimate getaway with seven spacious chalets built in Rungus style using local materials. A short walk leads down to the sea. The wide range of optional activities includes fishing, snorkelling, scuba diving, kayaking, boating, visiting traditional longhouses, massage etc, including transfers from Kota Kinabalu. Prices vary according to guest's requirements, with special rates for local visitors not requiring transport to the resort. RM120 Chatlet.

The Upper Deck Hotel

Jalan Lintas

Telephone: (088) 622 272, 622 282

A new hotel offering 24 rooms and 2 suites located on the top floor of a new building, overlooking Kudat Bay. All rooms have air-conditioning, attached bathroom, telephone, satellite TV and tea & coffee-making facilities. Prices from RM80 for a superior room to RM160 for a suite.

Hotel Kinabalu

Jalan Melor, Pekan Tomborungus

Telephone: (088) 613 888, 612 022

One of the older hotels conveniently located in Pekan Tomorungus, this offers 13 standard and 5 deluxe rooms, all with air-conditioning, attached bathroom, telephone and satellite TV, with refrigerators in the deluxe rooms. Prices range from RM42 to RM77 nett.

WHERE TO EAT

A large number of open, fan-cooled coffee shops in the old part of Kudat and Pekan Tomborungus offer a range of local food including Malay, Chinese, and Indian Muslim. There is also a fast-food fried chicken outlet in Pekan Tomorungus. Some of the more interesting places to eat include:

Tee Kim Ling

"No Name" Coffee Shop, located less than 1 km from the round-about and Shell station on Jalan Marudu. Open from 7 am until late afternoon, this famous spot for the Hakka speciality, *yong tau fu*, is in the second block of old wooden shophouses to the left, going out of Kudat. There is no name on the shop, which is between Yu Sin tailor and a refrigeration specialist. Excellent stuffed bean curd, egg rolls and other finely ground pork concoctions served in tasty broth with rice or noodles. Inexpensive. Closed on Sunday.

Sea View Gerai Makan, in the food stalls to the side of the Kudat Fish Market is open in the mornings for typical noodle dishes, but renowned for its seafood served in the evening. Diners can check the seafood and vegetables in the kitchen before deciding what they want and how they want it cooked. Some of the best dishes include steamed fish and claypot bean curd with mixed vegetables. Very reasonably priced, with inexpensive beer, young coconut juice and other drinks available.

Islamic Restaurant, Pekan Tomborungus
Perhaps the best place in Kudat to eat flaky fried Indian bread (*roti canai*).

Kedai Kopi Yu Hing, ground floor at the back of Hotel Ria
One of the newest, cleanest and brightest coffee shops in town, Yu Hing's corner location and small size helps keep it comfortably cool. Very good for breakfast, with delicious steamed buns (*pau*), a small range of *dim sum* and several types of noodles. Some of the best coffee in town, and a range of Chinese teas and other drinks. Also open for lunch but closed in the evening. Inexpensive.

Muslim Food Stalls, off Jalan Datu, near the Lembaga Bandaran Kudat
Early every evening, stall holders arrive at this open-air food centre to set out their cooked food or to start grilling fish, sting ray and chicken pieces. The grilled fish is usually sold with an optional local accompaniment, a roll of steamed tapioca starch. Simple and inexpensive. Only non-alcoholic beverages on sale.

Singgah Rasa, Kudat Rest House
Malay food and fresh fruit juice available for breakfast, lunch and dinner, either inside the restaurant or at outdoor tables. Moderately priced.

Sungai Wang Restaurant, Pekan Tomborungus
The most popular Chinese restaurant in town, this is usually quite busy. There is an open-sided dining area as well as a spacious air-conditioned room. Comprehensive menu with the usual range of dishes, with plenty of seafood. Moderately priced; beer and other drinks are available.

"Ah Foo" at the Kudat Golf Club
A very popular food and drink outlet at the Kudat Golf Club not only for golfers but also open to the general public and visitors to Kudat.

National Parks
of SARAWAK
Hans P. Hazebroek and Abang Kashim bin Abang Morshidi
Natural History Publications (Borneo)

A Walk through the
LOWLAND RAIN FOREST
of Sabah
Elaine J.F. Campbell

PREFERRED CHECK-LIST OF
SABAH TREES
Third Edition
Y.F. LEE
Natural History Publications (Borneo)

THE LARGER FUNGI
OF BORNEO
David N. Pegler
Natural History Publications

RAFFLESIA
OF THE WORLD
JAMILI NAIS

PITCHER-PLANTS
OF BORNEO
Anthea Phillipps and Anthony Lamb
with watercolour paintings by Susan M. Phillipps
and a Foreword by Tan Jiew Hoe

NEPENTHES
of BORNEO
CHARLES CLARKE
Natural History Publications

A GUIDE TO THE
Pitcher Plants
of Sabah
Charles Clarke
Natural History Publications (Borneo)

A GUIDE TO THE
Pitcher Plants of
Peninsular Malaysia
Charles Clarke
Natural History Publications (Borneo)

NEPENTHES
OF SUMATRA
AND PENINSULAR MALAYSIA
Charles Clarke
Natural History Publications (Borneo)

ORCHIDS
of SARAWAK
TEOFILA E. BEAMAN, JEFFREY J. WOOD,
REED S. BEAMAN AND JOHN H. BEAMAN
Natural History Publications (Borneo)
The Royal Botanic Gardens, Kew

ORCHIDS
of SUMATRA
J.B. Comber
Natural History Publications (Borneo)
The Royal Botanic Gardens, Kew

DENDROCHILUM
OF BORNEO
Jeffrey J. Wood
Natural History Publications (Borneo)
in association with
The Royal Botanic Gardens, Kew

THE PLANTS of
MOUNT KINABALU
3. GYMNOSPERMS AND NON-ORCHID MONOCOTYLEDONS
John H. Beaman and Reed S. Beaman
Natural History Publications (Borneo)
in association with
The Royal Botanic Gardens, Kew

THE PLANTS of
MOUNT KINABALU
4. DICOTYLEDON FAMILIES ACANTHACEAE TO LYTHRACEAE
John H. Beaman, Christiane Anderson and Reed S. Beaman
Natural History Publications (Borneo)
in association with
The Royal Botanic Gardens, Kew

The Genus
PAPHIOPEDILUM
Second Edition
Phillip Cribb
Natural History Publications (Borneo)
in association with
The Royal Botanic Gardens, Kew

SLIPPER ORCHIDS OF BORNEO
Phillip Cribb
Natural History Publications

THE GENUS COELOGYNE
A SYNOPSIS
Dudley Clayton
Natural History Publications (Borneo)
in association with
The Royal Botanic Gardens, Kew

GINGERS
of PENINSULAR MALAYSIA AND SINGAPORE
K. Larsen, H. Ibrahim, S.H. Khaw and L.G. Saw
Natural History Publications (Borneo)

MOSSES AND LIVERWORTS of MOUNT KINABALU
Jan Peter Frahm, Wolfgang Frey,
Harald Kürschner and Mario Menzel

PHASMIDS of BORNEO
Philip E. Bragg
Natural History Publications (Borneo)

An Illustrated Guide to the
STICK AND LEAF INSECTS
of Peninsular Malaysia and Singapore
FRANCIS SEOW-CHOEN
Natural History Publications (Borneo)
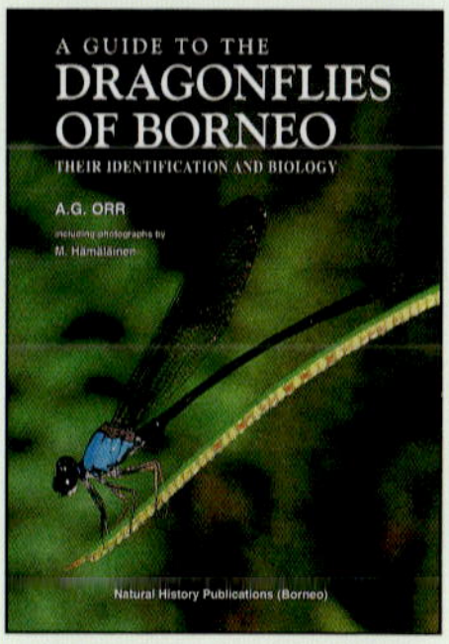
A GUIDE TO THE
DRAGONFLIES OF BORNEO
THEIR IDENTIFICATION AND BIOLOGY
A.G. ORR
including photographs by
M. Hämäläinen
Natural History Publications (Borneo)
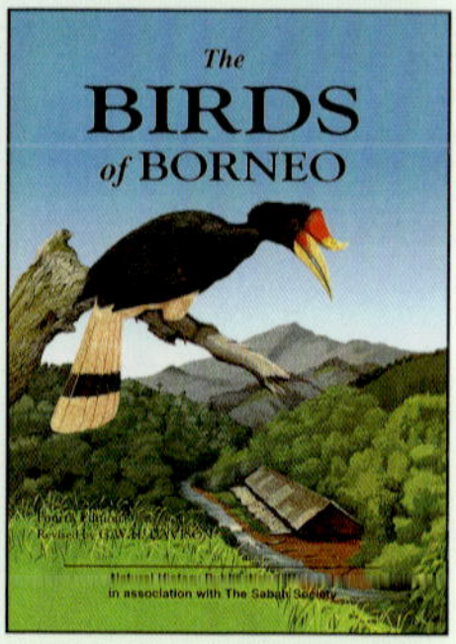
The BIRDS of BORNEO
in association with The Sabah Society

The BIRDS of BURMA
Fourth Edition
Bertram E. Smythies
Natural History Publications (Borneo)

Swiftlets of Borneo
BUILDERS OF EDIBLE NESTS
Lim Chan Koon and Earl of Cranbrook
Natural History Publications (Borneo)

The Natural History of
ORANG-UTAN
Elizabeth L. Bennett
Natural History Publications (Borneo)

PROBOSCIS MONKEYS OF BORNEO
Elizabeth L. Bennett and Francis Gombek

A Field Guide to the
FROGS OF BORNEO
Robert F. Inger
Robert B. Stuebing

The Natural History of
AMPHIBIANS AND REPTILES IN SABAH
Robert F. Inger and Tan Fui Lian

An Introduction to the
Amphibians and Reptiles of Tropical Asia
Indraneil Das
Natural History Publications (Borneo)

A FIELD GUIDE TO THE
SNAKES of BORNEO
Robert B. Stuebing and Robert F. Inger
Natural History Publications (Borneo)

Man-eating
CROCODILES
of Borneo
JAMES RITCHIE
with JOHNSON JONG
Natural History Publications (Borneo)

TURTLES
of BORNEO
AND PENINSULAR MALAYSIA
Lim Boo Liat and Indraneil Das
Natural History Publications (Borneo)

MARINE FOOD FISHES
AND FISHERIES
OF SABAH
Chin Phui Kong
Natural History Publications

THE
FRESH-WATER FISHES
OF NORTH BORNEO
ROBERT F. INGER AND CHIN PHUI KONG
Natural History Publications (Borneo)

LAYANG LAYANG
A Drop in the Ocean
Nicolas Pilcher, Steve Oakley and Ghazally Ismail
Natural History Publications (Borneo)

THREE
CAME HOME
Agnes N. Keith
Natural History Publications

Land Below The Wind
Agnes Newton Keith
Natural History Publications (Borneo)

WHITE MAN
RETURNS
Agnes Newton Keith
With an Introduction by Patricia Regis
Natural History Publications (Borneo)

WITH THE WILD MEN OF
BORNEO
Elizabeth Mershon
Natural History Publications (Borneo)

FOREST LIFE AND ADVENTURES
IN THE
MALAY ARCHIPELAGO
Eric Mjöberg
Natural History Publications (Borneo)

A NATURALIST
IN BORNEO
Robert W.C. Shelford
Natural History Publications (Borneo)

TWENTY YEARS
IN BORNEO
Charles Bruce
Natural History Publications (Borneo)

The
DRAGON
of Kinabalu
and other Borneo Stories
Owen Rutter
Natural History Publications (Borneo)

A CULTURAL HERITAGE OF NORTH BORNEO
Animal Tales
of Sabah
P. S. Shim
with illustrations by Yong Ket Hyun
Natural History Publications (Borneo)

Kadazan
Folklore
Compiled and edited by
Rita Lasimbang
Illustrated by
Suzie Majikol
Natural History Publications (Borneo)

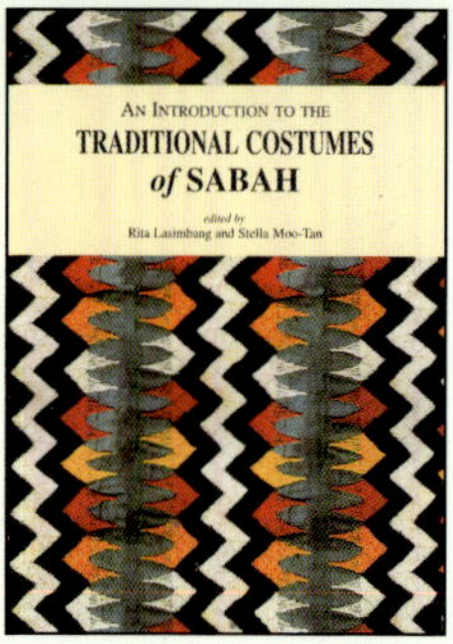
AN INTRODUCTION TO THE
TRADITIONAL COSTUMES
of SABAH
edited by
Rita Lasimbang and Stella Moo-Tan